Helping Young Children With Phonics

ACKNOWLEDGEMENTS

Written by: Ros Bayley & Lynn Broadbent

Illustrated by: Peter Scott

Produced & Published by: Lawrence Educational
                          PO Box 532, Cambridge, CB1 0BX, UK

© Lawrence Educational 2002

ISBN: 978-1-903670-13-2

Introduction

This publication has been written to help busy early years practitioners bring additional engagement and excitement to their programme of work for phonics. The activities revolve around a mischievous crow called Crispin, a puppet that is easy to manipulate and also extremely vocal! Using some very simple story scenarios, Crispin can be used to create an exciting context for a wide variety of phonic activities. Each activity is simply laid out and uses easily available resources. At the end of each activity links are made with Progression in Phonics.

Introducing Crispin

These activities use the power of puppets and story to support children in the learning process. Crispin the mischievous crow will quickly capture the children's imagination and ensure that they are engaged at an emotional level. This in turn, will lead to deeper learning.

To create the appropriate 'magic,' you could take Crispin in wrapped in a pillowcase. Tell the children you have brought a friend for them to meet. Jerk the pillowcase to make it look alive and give it a little press to make Crispin give a little squawk!

Slowly and with a great sense of occasion, bring Crispin out of the bag. If you feel at all self conscious about doing this, practice in front of a mirror! This will help you to see how to move the puppet to greatest advantage! Experiment with his 'squeaker.' With a little practice you can make a wide variety of sounds, ranging from small and plaintive to loud and outrageous. Where possible, it is useful to work with another adult, as this enables one to concentrate on manipulating the puppet while the other one works directly with the children. Once the children have had a chance to meet Crispin and speculate on where he has come from, use these activities in whatever way most meets your needs.

Most of the activities can be used more than once in a variety of ways, and how you use them will depend on the developmental stage of the children you are working with. Exactly how you use this programme will be determined by your professional judgement.

Keeping Crispin's Magic Alive

Crispin is the practitioners puppet. He is not intended for the children to play with and you will need to find a way of keeping him 'special.' Once a session is over, replace him in a bag or box and put him away until the next session. Used in this way his appeal will grow and grow as the children build up a rapport with him. In fact, the more you use him, the more popular he will become!

Ros Bayley & Lynn Broadbent

Activity 1

Crispin's Collection

This activity can be used to focus the children's attention on identifying different phonemes in either the initial, or final position.

Resources:
A variety of objects beginning with the same initial/final phoneme plus some objects that don't 'fit.'

Process:

1. Explain to the children that Crispin likes to collect things and that he has made a collection and hidden the things he has collected all over the place and forgotten where he has put them. (Prior to this you will need to hide the collection of items in the classroom or in the outside area.)

2. Show the children photographs or pictures of the things he has collected. Alternatively make a list on a whiteboard and ask them what they notice about the collection. For example, that most things begin with 's' or 't'.

3. Have a grand search and as each item is found it can be checked off against the list. (Crispin can screech in appreciation.)

4. Once the items have been found the children can show Crispin how to write the phoneme/phonemes you are focusing on.)

5. The children can then collect additional items for Crispin's collection.

Activity 2

Crispin's Magic Paintbrush

This activity can be used to focus on initial, final or dominant phonemes.

Resources:
A paintbrush, which has been made to look special, e.g. paint it gold or silver or decorate it with moons and stars.
A list of words on a whiteboard/flipchart with specific phoneme missing e.g. initial

Process:
1. Tell the children that Crispin has got hold of a magic paintbrush and used it to make a lot of phonemes disappear. Explain that before they came into school you wrote a list of words on the whiteboard/flipchart but that when you came back to look at them Crispin had been up to his tricks.

2. Show the children the magic paintbrush. (Crispin can look suitably embarrassed!)

3. Get the children to write the missing phonemes in the right places. Crispin will of course express his thanks!

4. Alternatively, give each child a magnetic letter and support them to place it correctly.

Activity 3

Crispin Goes Shopping

This activity can be used to promote work across a range of learning objectives and can be adapted for a range of purposes.

Resources:
A shopping basket/bag packed with a range of items. (Exactly what you put in the bag will be determined by your objective.)

Process:
1. Explain to the children that Crispin has been to the supermarket and 'helped himself' to a wide variety of items that will now have to be returned.

2. Pass the shopping around the children and let them take an item out of the bag. Get the children to name the item as they take it out. Ask them what they notice about these items e.g. that they all begin with 'b' or some begin with 's' and some with 'w.' If there are a range of items see if the children can group themselves according to the item they have selected or been given. Use hoops, 'stations' or labels to assist the children in this task. If appropriate arrange the group of things alphabetically.

3. Make a list of all the things that Crispin has collected in the supermarket. Explain to the children that having them sorted in this way will help the supermarket manager to know exactly what Crispin has taken out of the shop. The children can show Crispin how to write the initial phonemes (and more if they are able.)

4. Crispin can thank the children for all their hard work.

Activity 4

Crispin's Toy Box

This activity can be used to support children in hearing and saying initial phonemes. It can also be adapted for a variety of other learning objectives.

Resources:
A range of toys gathered from around the setting.
(Your selection will be guided by the phonemes on which you wish to focus

Process:
1. Explain to the children that Crispin has been trying to sort his toys out according to the phoneme with which they begin, but that he has got stuck and got them all muddled up.

2. Sit the children in a circle with the toys in the middle. Ask them for their ideas about how best to sort the toys out and then group them accordingly.

3. If appropriate, make a list for Crispin. The children can show him how to write the initial phonemes.

Activity 5

The Jumble Sale

This activity can be adapted for use across a range of purposes and manipulated to meet a variety of learning objectives.

Resources:
A range of articles with some simple CVC names e.g. cat, dog, bus, man, pot, pen, hat, nut, peg, pig, car, tin etc.
Some labels/price tags to match the items.

Process:
1. Explain to the children that a friend of yours had arranged her stall for the local jumble sale then gone for a cup of tea. While she was away Crispin had picked everything up and replaced it in the box.

2. Distribute the items and the labels and get the children to sort them out. Alternatively, if developmentally appropriate, get them to write new labels or a price list for the jumble sale stall.

3. Ask the children what they notice about the labels, encouraging them to notice similarities and differences.

Activity 6   # Crispin and the Magnetic Letters

This activity can be used as a means of focusing on phonemes in an initial, medial or final position or for CVC blending, segmenting reading and spelling.

Resources:
Magnetic letters and a board.

Process:

1. Prior to this activity put up a CVC rhyming string on the board with the magnetic letters but have some of them missing (e.g. initial, medial or final.)

2. Explain to the children that Crispin has interfered with the display and pulled off some of the letters and either hidden them or dropped them somewhere.

3. Once the letters have been retrieved the children can help Crispin to put them back in the right place. Crispin will of course be suitably appreciative and will squawk wildly when a letter is correctly placed.

Activity 7

Crispin's Birthday Presents

This activity will help children to hear and say phonemes in the initial position and practice phoneme/grapheme correspondences.

Resources:
Items that have been gift wrapped and labelled with their initial phoneme.

Process:
1. Tell the children that it is Crispin's birthday and that he has got some presents to open. Explain that before he opens them he wants the children to help him to try and guess what is inside the parcels.

2. Sit the children in a circle and pass the presents round so that they can make their guesses.

3. Once the children have made their guesses, open the presents and see how many they got right.

4. The children can show Crispin how to write the initial letters to match the presents.

Activity 8

Crispin Visits the Safari Park

This activity focuses on initial phonemes and phoneme /grapheme correspondence.

Resources:
Pictures of animals (these will be determined by what phonemes you wish to focus on.)

Process:
1. Tell the children that Crispin has been to the Safari Park and would like to show the children some pictures of the animals he saw when he was there.

2. Give out the letter cards and explain to the children that as Crispin shows them each picture they are to say the initial phoneme and hold up the letter card.

3. The children can then show Crispin how to write each phoneme on the whiteboard or flipchart.

Activity 9

Crispin Gives Everyone a Phoneme

This activity focuses on initial phonemes and phoneme/grapheme correspondence.

Resources:
A collection of artefacts and phoneme cards.

Process:
1. Get the children to sit in a circle then place a letter card face down in front of each child.

2. Place an artefact in the middle of the circle and if the children have a card that corresponds to the initial phoneme of the artefact they place it next to it.

3. Crispin squawks appreciatively if they are all correct. If they are not he shakes his head slowly and the children check to see which cards have been incorrectly placed.

Activity 10

What's in Crispin's Bag?

This activity requires the children to segment to spell CVC words.

Resources:
Some objects that can be labelled with simple CVC words e.g. toy, dog, car, cat, tin, hat, pot, cup, lid, mug etc.
A large bag to put them in.
A whiteboard for each child (if appropriate.) Alternatively you could use letter cards.

Process:

1. Explain to the children that Crispin wants to make a list of all the things in his bag and that he needs their help to do it.

2. As you draw each item from the bag the children make a list for Crispin.

3. Crispin squawks his appreciation when the list is complete.

4. The children can then read back the words as the bag is packed.

Activity 11

What Has Crispin Lost?

This activity focuses on blending to read CVC words.

Resources:
Some objects that can be labelled with simple CVC words e.g. toy, dog, car, cat, man, hat, pot, cup, lid, mug, tin etc.
A list that corresponds to the objects with some extra objects on the list (these are the ones that Crispin has lost.)

Process:
1. Explain to the children that Crispin has lost some of the things from his collection but he doesn't know which ones are missing. In order to find out he needs to check the items off against the list.

2. Get the children to read the list and check that the items are there. They can then tell Crispin the ones that are missing.

How Do You Write It?

This activity requires the children to segment to spell CVC words.

Resources:
Some objects that can be named using simple CVC words e.g. hat, cup, lid, mug, dog, cat, man, tin etc. (Alternatively you could use picture cards.

Process:

1. The children sit in a circle.

2. Crispin chooses an item or a picture to place in the bag but does so without the children seeing.

3. The bag is passed round the circle until Crispin squawks. The person who is holding the bag then removes the item for everyone to see.

4. The children show Crispin how to write the word.

Crispin Rubs It Out

This activity is an adaptation of the Magic Paintbrush and requires the children to read simple CVC words and write final phonemes. (It can also be adapted for medial and final phonemes.)

Resources:
A whiteboard and a cloth or rubber.

Process:

1. Write a list of words with the final phoneme missing.

2. Bring Crispin out of his bag and then bring out the marker or rubber from the bottom of his bag.

3. Crispin hangs his head in shame as you explain that he has rubbed the final letter off every word on your list!

4. The children help you to identify and write the missing letter.

Activity 14

Crispin Plays With The Pointer

This activity requires the children to hear and say initial phonemes.

Resources:

A large poster e.g. from the seaside etc.   (The subject you choose will be dictated by the phonemes you wish to focus on.)
Letter cards.

Process:

1.   Crispin holds the pointer and then points to a feature on the poster.

2.   The children say the initial phoneme of the thing that Crispin has pointed to.

3.   If appropriate they can match the phoneme to the right letter card.

Activity 15

Crispin's Painted Stones

This game can be adapted for a variety of purposes.

Resources:
Some flat pebbles or stones with phonemes painted on them. A 'conch' or something similar for passing.

Process:

1. The children sit in a circle and the 'conch' is passed round until Crispin 'caws.'

2. The child holding the 'conch' then selects a pebble. They could do this at random, and then the other children can think of something beginning with that phoneme, or they could have to select a stone that fulfils the criteria set by the practitioner.

   - Alternatively, they might select the appropriate stone for segmenting and spelling CVC words.

Activity 16

Crispin and the Post-Its

This activity can be used to help children with phoneme-grapheme correspondences or for blending and reading CVC words.

Resources:
A packet of post-its, a 'conch' or 'talking stick.'

Process:

1. Write some phonemes on the post-its.

2. Sit the children in a circle and pass round the conch. When Crispin 'caws' the person holding the conch rips off a post-it and displays it for everyone to see.

3. The conch is then passed around again and as each child gets it they say the name of something beginning with that phoneme.

4. You can also write phonemes that will build into CVC or CCVC words to give practice with blending and reading.

Activity 17

Change Seats

This activity can be used and adapted for a range of purposes.

Resources:

Picture cards, phoneme cards or cards with simple CVC words.

Process:

1.   The children sit in a circle and the practitioner shouts out instructions. For example:
     - All those children that have a picture beginning with 'm' change seats.
     - All those children that have a word with an 'a' in the middle change seats.
     - All those children that have a word that ends with 'n' change seats.

Activity 18

Crispin's Musical Chairs

This activity can be adapted for a range of purposes.

Resources:
A line of chairs arranged as for a game of musical chairs.
Pictures, phonemes or simple CVC words that can be blue-tac'd to the seats of the chairs.

Process:

- The children move around the chairs and when Crispin 'caws' everyone sits down

- Crispin then chooses some children to name their phoneme/read what is on their chair.

  Alternatively, if you are working with a group, the children can take turns to name their phoneme/read their word.

Activity 19

Pass It On

This game can be adapted for a range of purposes.

Resources:
Objects, phoneme cards or simple CVC words.

Process:
1. The children sit in a circle and the objects or cards are distributed (one for each child.)

2. When Crispin 'caws'

3. The objects are passed around the circle.
   (If the children find this difficult they can pass on the 'caw.')

4. After a few 'passes' the children group themselves according to given criteria. For example:
   - Everyone who has something beginning with 't' make a group.
   - Everyone who has a word with an 'o' in the middle make a group.

Activity 20

Time to Wake Up Crispin

This game can be adapted for a range of purposes.

Resources:
Objects, pictures or phoneme cards (one for each child.)   A 'conch' or similar item for passing round.

Process:
1. The children sit in a circle and the objects, pictures or cards are distributed.
2. Pass the 'conch' around and on a given signal (it can't be made by Crispin because he's fast asleep!) the children stop.
3. The person holding the 'conch' shows their object or card and the other children with the same object or card identify themselves.
4. The group then begin to say that phoneme, first very quietly then getting gradually louder until Crispin finally wakes up!
5. He then falls asleep again and the 'conch' is passed around for a second time (or a third or fourth, until Crispin is finally wide awake!)

Activity 21

Crispin's Picnic

This activity is intended to support children to learn grapheme/phoneme correspondences.

Resources:
Picture cards of food, fruit etc that Crispin is going to take on his picnic. Phoneme cards.

Process:
1. The children sit in a circle and the picture cards are given out.

2. One by one Crispin picks phoneme cards from his bag or box.

3. If the children are holding a picture card where the item begins with the same sound they give it to Crispin, who then expresses his appreciation.

Activity 22

How Well Does Crispin Do?

The activity can be adapted for a range of purposes.

Resources:
A phoneme chart, a pointer for Crispin (unless he decides to use his beak!)

Process:

1. The children sit I a circle and the 'conch' is passed around.

2. On a given signal the person holding the 'conch' selects a picture from the picture card box and shows it to Crispin and the rest of the children.

3. Crispin points to the phoneme that corresponds to the object.

4. The children put their thumbs up if they think he has pointed correctly or make the thumbs down sign if they think he has got it wrong.

Activity 23

Crispin's Phoneme Tree

This activity is intended to help children hear and say initial or final phonemes and know phoneme/grapheme correspondences.

Resources:
Some branches cut from a tree and stuck into buckets of sand or flowerpots filled with quick drying cement.
Some picture cards that can be hung on the branches of a tree.

Process:
1. The children sit in a circle with the 'trees' in the middle and the picture cards are distributed (at least one for each child.)

2. A large label representing an initial or final phoneme is placed by the tree.

3. Those children who have a picture where the phoneme corresponds to the label hang their picture in the tree and take another card.

4. A new label is placed by the tree and the activity is repeated. It can be repeated as many times as you wish.

Activity 24

Crispin's Mystery words

This activity can be adapted for a variety of purposes but it is especially useful for blending and reading CVC words.

Resources:
A list of words written on a whiteboard and some post-its with which to reveal the letters.

Process:

1. Tell the children that Crispin has set them a task and written some words on the whiteboard to see if they can read them.

2. As you reveal the letters get the children to think about and try to predict what letter will be next or what the final phoneme might be. Use Crispin to respond to their predictions. He can become very excited or shake his head if they are on the wrong track!

3. Once the words have been revealed and read see if they can be reorganised to make a message e.g. I saw a man and a dog on the hill.

Crispin's Rhyming Strings

The activity is intended to help children continue a rhyming string.

Resources:
A roll of paper and a marker pen.
An impressive piece of ribbon.

Process:

1. Explain to the children that Crispin needs some help to make some rhyming strings.

2. Show them the roll of paper and tell them that you will write them down for him as the children think of them.

3. Crispin whispers the first word of the rhyming string in your ear and once you have shared this with the children they take turns to add to the string.

4. Once completed it is rolled up, tied with ribbon and presented to Crispin who shows his appreciation.

Activity 26

Crispin Goes For A Walk

This activity is useful for blending and reading, segmenting and spelling CVC words.

Resources:
Some objects, words or picture cards of things that can be labelled using CVC words.
A 'conch' or similar for passing round.

Process:
1. Explain to the children that Crispin has been for a long walk and that on the way he has collected lots of different things. Tell them that they are going to help him to make a list of all those things.

2. The children sit in a circle and the conch is passed around. When Crispin 'caws' the person holding the conch selects an object from the box.

3. The children work together to write the word on the whiteboard and then the conch is passed around again until the list is complete.

Crispin And The Missing Letters

This activity is intended to help children hear, say and know phoneme/grapheme correspondences in CVC words and to support them with segmenting and spelling.

Resources:
A list of words with either the initial, medial or final phoneme missing. (For some children it is useful to have a picture by the side of the word.) A phoneme card for each child with one of the missing letters written on it.

Process:
1. The children look at the first word on the list and try to work out which phoneme is missing.

2. Once they have decided on the most appropriate one, they show their letters to Crispin and he indicates which one he wants (which could be correct or incorrect!)

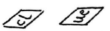

Activity 28

Crispin's Disappearing Words

This activity provides children with opportunities for blending and reading CVC words.

Resources:
A permanent marker, some balloons and a 'conch' for passing round.

Process:
1. Write some CVC words on the balloons <u>before</u> they are blown up.

2. The children sit in a circle and the conch is passed round. When Crispin 'caws' the child holding the conch selects a balloon and reads (or is supported to read) the word.

3. The balloon is then blown up (which makes the word almost disappear – at the very least it becomes very faint.)

4. The children try to remember how to write the word and write it on the whiteboard.

Activity 29   # Crispin's String of Handkerchiefs

This activity can be adapted for a range of purposes.

Resources:
Some white handkerchiefs, or pieces of white material and something to put them in. (A tube of cardboard works well!)
Objects or picture cards.

Process:

1. Prior to the session write some phonemes or words on the handkerchiefs. Knot them together and stuff them into the tube magician style.

2. Sit the children in a circle and give out the objects or the picture cards.

3. As Crispin pulls the hankies out of the tube the children look to see if the phoneme matches their picture or object.

Activity 30

Crispin and the Disappearing Ink

This activity can be adapted for a range of purposes.

Resources:

Some marker pens and some disappearing ink! (This is easily available from any Joke shop.)

Process:

1. Write a phoneme or word using Crispin's disappearing ink and watch it disappear. (This ensures that the children pay close attention to the letter or word as they really enjoy observing this process.)

2. Once the phoneme or word has disappeared the children show Crispin how to write it again, this time using a marker pen.

3. They can then help him to find pictures, objects or words to match the one on the whiteboard.

We hope you have found this publication useful. Other books in our 'Helping Young Children' series are:

Helping Young Children with STEADY BEAT	978-1-903670-26-2
Helping Young Children with PHONOLOGICAL AWARENESS	978-1-903670-73-6
Helping Young Children with NUMERACY	978-1-903670-20-0
Helping Young Children with PHONICS	978-1-903670-13-2
Helping Young Children LEARN TO READ	978-1-903670-32-3
Helping Young Children to SPEAK WITH CONFIDENCE	978-1-903670-33-0
Helping Young Children to LISTEN	978-1-903670-04-0
Helping Young Children to CONCENTRATE	978-1-903670-29-3
Helping Young Children to COME TO THEIR SENSES	978-1-903670-57-6
Helping Young Children to IMAGINE	978-1-903670-12-5
Helping Young Children to THINK CREATIVELY	978-1-903670-14-9
Helping Young Children to LEARN THROUGH MOVEMENT	978-1-903670-34-7
Helping Young Children with PSE through story	978-1-903670-45-3
Helping Young Children to ASK QUESTIONS	978-1-903670-36-1

For further information about these and our other publications, visit our website:

www.LawrenceEducational.co.uk